HODDER ENGLISH GOLD

Romeo and Juliet

The aim of this book is to help you to find out more about Shakespeare's *Romeo and Juliet*. You need to understand the play as a whole. To do this:

- You will follow the plot by looking at events in all five acts
- You will study the characters and the parts they play in events
- You will think about and discuss the characters' reasons for behaving as they do.

  You will develop your skills as:

SPEAKERS AND LISTENERS

by taking part in role-play, 'hot seating' and other activities
by discussing the characters

READERS

by reading some of the original text
by finding evidence in the text to support your ideas
by exploring images

WRITERS

by re-writing some of the text in modern English
by explaining your ideas clearly in more detail
by producing longer pieces of writing for coursework

ROLE-PLAY CARDS

The aim of this activity is to explore the main themes of the play. The role-play cards introduce some of the themes and issues in *Romeo and Juliet.* You will need to work in groups.

- Each card describes a situation. Read this and discuss it in your group.

- Then role-play the situation and show the other groups what happens.

- Discuss your role-play with the rest of the class. Talk about:
  - what the characters did;
  - how the characters reacted – did they do the right thing?

HELP

There is no need to write a script. It is better to make it up as you go along. This is called 'improvising'.

ROLE-PLAY CARD
CARD A   (Group of 4–5)

Background:
For some time you have been seeing a girl your family likes. You like her and feel she is right for you.

What's happening:
You are at a disco. You see a girl across the room you don't know. You feel drawn to her. You ask her to dance but she says 'No'. You are very upset. You go back to your friends who wonder why you are upset.

ROLE-PLAY CARD
CARD B   (Group of 4–5)

Background:
You usually like to be with your mates. You often meet up with them and play football or music. Recently they have begun to go to parties and discos. You are not very keen on parties.

What's happening:
It is the weekend and your mates want to go to a party. You are not keen. They try to persuade you to go.

Romeo *Juliet*

ROLE-PLAY CARD
CARD C   (Group of 2–4)

Background:
Your parents don't mind you going out but are strict about the time you should be in.

What's happening:
You have been to a party. You are late getting home. Your parents are waiting up for you and they are not pleased.

Romeo *Juliet*

ROLE-PLAY CARD
CARD D   (Group of 5–6)

Background:
Your neighbours are a couple with no children. They do not like noise. You are one of four students who live next to them.

What's happening:
You've just bought the latest dance CD. You and your friends are listening to it. It is loud. There is a loud knock at the door. You open it to find your neighbour standing there.

Romeo *Juliet*

ROLE-PLAY CARD
CARD E   (Group of 2-6)

Background:
You are jealous because a person new to the school has got into the school netball/football team. This means you are left out.

What's happening:
You are in the playground at lunchtime. The new person is there talking to a friend. You are mad and go over to start a fight or an argument.

Romeo *Juliet*

ROLE-PLAY CARD
CARD F   (Group of 2-3)

Background:
You are usually good at attending school. However, things have got on top of you in the last few weeks so you have fallen behind with your work. You have not done your homework.

What's happening:
You are not going to school and pretend to be ill. Instead you will meet a close friend and have fun for the day.

THE PROLOGUE

Shakespeare starts his play with a prologue which tells the audience what will happen. Compare Shakespeare's prologue with a modern version.

The prologue	Modern version
Enter chorus Two households, both alike in dignity, In fair Verona (where we lay our scene), From ancient grudge break to new mutiny, Where civil blood makes civil hands unclean. From forth the fatal loins of these two foes A pair of star-crossed lovers take their life; Whose misadventured piteous overthrows Doth with their death bury their parents' strife.	Two families that are the same in every way, live in Verona where our play takes place. An old quarrel exists and now a new fight erupts and people have been killed. The children of these two enemies are destined to fall in love and kill themselves; and their sad deaths lead to the end of their parents' quarrel.

- Look at how the language changes:
  alike – the same
  ancient grudge – old quarrel
  foes – enemies
  star-crossed lovers – destined to fall in love
- Now see if you can put together a modern version of the last six lines of the prologue from the lines below. Get your teacher to help you if you get stuck.

The fearful passage of their death-marked love,
And the continuance of their parents' rage,
Which but their children's end nought could remove,
Is now the two hours' traffic of our stage;
The which if you with patient ears attend,
What here shall miss, our toil shall strive to mend.

FAMILY PORTRAIT ALBUM

PREDICTING THE PLAY

- Discuss:

1 What might the quarrel be about?

2 How might the children die?

Look to see if there are any clues in the text.

DISCUSSION POINT

What might the 'ancient grudge' be about? Why do families argue?

The Montague family

The Capulet family

READING THE PLAY

The play is divided into five separate parts called acts. We are now going to look at Act One. You can understand the basic storyline by following the cartoon. Try to watch a film version of Act One and read some of the original text.

ACT ONE

Verona: the Montagues and Capulets are fighting again …

Prince Escalus arrives and warns the crowd that anyone caught fighting again will be sentenced to death.

A sad Romeo, who has missed the fight, talks to his friend Benvolio.

Romeo and Benvolio discover that the Capulets are having a party. Benvolio talks Romeo into going.

That evening, Romeo and his mates disguise themselves with masks and gatecrash the Capulet party.

At the party, Romeo and Juliet fall in love as soon as they see each other.

At the end of the party Romeo and Juliet learn one another's identity.

IDENTIFYING THE CHARACTERS

Can you identify these characters? Remember to start with a capital letter when you write their names. Look back at the family photographs and the cartoon version of Act One.

INVITATIONS

In the play Lord Capulet sends a servant to invite people to his party. Imagine you have been asked to design an invitation for him. Look at the following examples, then design and fill in the details on your own invitation.

It's party time! So come and dine with the Capulets tonight, at

Dear _____

You are invited to a party

on _____

at _____

beginning at _____

RSVP

Lord and Lady Capulet

have great pleasure in inviting

_____

to their annual feast

ACT TWO

Later that night Romeo listens beneath Juliet's window.

Romeo and Juliet tell each other about their love, and talk of marriage.

Very early the next morning Romeo finds Friar Lawrence and asks for his help.

Later that morning, Benvolio and Mercutio talk about Tybalt, who is upset that Romeo gatecrashed the party. They suspect that Tybalt has challenged Romeo to a duel.

Juliet sends her nurse to find out from Romeo about the arrangements for their marriage.

Back at the Capulet mansion the nurse gives Romeo's message to Juliet.

Later, at Friar Lawrence's cell, Romeo and Juliet are married in secret.

KEY MOMENTS IN ACT TWO

- You are going to use role-play cards again. This will help you to understand Act Two. These cards are a little different to the others. You will need to work with a partner, because each role-play card involves two characters.

- On each card is a description of a scene and some background information.

1 Think about the characters in the scene and what they might say. Use the background information to help you.

2 Decide which character would say the line on the card. Include this in your role-play.

3 Now role-play the scene.

Romeo *Juliet*

ROLE-PLAY CARD
CARD 1   Romeo & Juliet

Juliet is on her balcony. She talks to herself about her love for Romeo. Romeo has been listening and now reveals himself. What do they say?

Earlier that evening they met for the first time and fell in love. After the party they discovered that their families were enemies.

'Art thou not Romeo, and a Montague?'

Romeo *Juliet*

ROLE-PLAY CARD
CARD 2   Romeo & Friar Lawrence

It is very early in the morning. Romeo has not been to bed. Romeo tells Friar Lawrence that he wants to marry Juliet. Romeo asks Friar Lawrence to perform the wedding today. What do they say?

They are good friends and last time Friar Lawrence saw him, Romeo claimed he was in love with another girl called Rosaline. Friar Lawrence has to weigh up the pros and cons of doing what Romeo asks.

'Holy Saint Francis! What a change is here!'

Romeo & Juliet

ROLE-PLAY CARD

CARD 3   Benvolio and Mercutio
(Romeo's friends)

The morning after the party they still can't find Romeo. They hear that Tybalt (a Capulet) has sent a letter to Romeo and assume that he has challenged him to a duel. What do they say?

They do not know that Romeo has met Juliet. Tybalt was very upset about Romeo gate-crashing the party. Tybalt is an expert swordsman.

'Where the devil should this Romeo be? Came he not home tonight?'

Romeo & Juliet

ROLE-PLAY CARD

CARD 4   The nurse & Romeo

Juliet has sent the nurse to find Romeo. Romeo tells her when and where the wedding will take place. It is to be a secret and no one else must know about their plans. What do they say?

The nurse and Friar Lawrence are the only people who know about Romeo and Juliet's plans to get married.

'What wilt thou tell her, nurse?'

Romeo & Juliet

ROLE-PLAY CARD

CARD 5   Juliet & the nurse

The nurse returns to Juliet with a message from Romeo. She has been a long time and Juliet can't wait to hear her news. The nurse teases Juliet by keeping back what Romeo said. What do they say?

The nurse is Juliet's closest friend and is in on the secret. She enjoys a joke.

'Sweet, sweet, sweet nurse, tell me, what says my love?'

Romeo & Juliet

ROLE-PLAY CARD

CARD 6   Romeo & Friar Lawrence

Juliet must pretend that she is going to confession that afternoon. Instead she is to meet Romeo in secret at Friar Lawrence's cell where they will be married. Romeo and Friar Lawrence wait for her. What do they say?

Romeo and Juliet are madly in love. Although they only met less than 24 hours ago they can't wait to be married. Friar Lawrence still has some worries about how quickly everything is happening.

'These violent delights have violent ends.'

A TIMELESS STORY

Shakespeare's play *Romeo and Juliet* has fascinated many
artists. It has been made into films and musicals, and has
inspired paintings and songs. How many versions of the play
or references to it do you know?

DISCUSSION POINT

Why do you think *Romeo and Juliet* is still a popular play today?

THE CAPULET PARTY

Imagine you have been asked to design costumes for Act One, Scene Five, where Romeo and Juliet meet for the first time. Look at the costumes shown here, and discuss the following:

- The Capulets are very rich and this is an important occasion for them. In the versions shown, how do the costumes show this is an important occasion?

- When Romeo first sees Juliet he says 'O! she doth teach the torches to burn bright.' Juliet is often dressed in white and made to stand out from the crowd. Why is this? What words would remind you of the colour white? On what occasions is white worn and why?

- In the play Romeo and his friends put on masks before they enter the party. Capulet says his days for wearing masks are over. Why would the young men wear masks?

- Design your own costumes for Romeo and Juliet to wear in this scene. Will it be a modern version or something more traditional? You may want to do some research in the library first.

- Label your design clearly explaining your choice of colours and designs. Will Romeo wear a mask? Will Juliet stand out in the crowd? Write about your design explaining your choice and how it reflects the characters.

- Compare your design to those of previous productions.

THE BALCONY SCENE

You are now going to look more closely at the language in
Act Two, Scene Two: the balcony scene.

– Romeo listens beneath Juliet's window.
  She loves him and says that his name
  is not important.

– Romeo makes his presence known and
  climbs up to the balcony to talk to
  Juliet.

– They confess their love for each other.

– Juliet says if he means it he should
  arrange their marriage.

– Romeo says he will do this and send
  word to her tomorrow.

– They part.

There are some wonderful
romantic lines in this scene.

- Look at the following; who speaks
  each line and what do they mean?

- Practise different ways of saying each
  line, to bring out the meaning.

♥ 'O, that I were a glove upon that hand',
  That I might touch that cheek!'

♥ 'O, Romeo, Romeo! – Wherefore art
  thou Romeo?'

♥ 'That which we call a rose
  By any other word would smell as
  sweet.'

♥ 'My ears have yet not drunk a
  hundred words
  Of thy tongue's uttering,
  yet I know the sound.'

♥ 'This bud of love, by summer's
  ripening breath,
  May prove a beauteous flower when
  we next meet.'

♥ 'My bounty is as boundless as the sea,
  My love as deep.'

♥ 'I am afeard,
  Being in night, all this is but a dream.'

♥ 'Love goes toward love as schoolboys
  from their books;
  But love from love, toward school with
  heavy looks.'

- Read or watch the scene again to see
  if you were right.

- Now produce a class display by
  choosing one line from the scene and
  illustrating it.

ACT THREE, SCENE ONE

- Photocopy this page and cut the boxes out. The boxes are in the wrong order.

- Read the text carefully, then fit the pieces together.

- Then write or tell a partner what is happening in this scene.

Romeo now fights Tybalt …

Mercutio challenges Tybalt and they fight. Romeo tries to stop them.

Mercutio is wounded and dies.

The Prince banishes Romeo. He must leave Verona for ever.

and kills him.

Romeo runs away.

Verona, that afternoon. Tybalt tries to force Romeo to fight him but Romeo refuses.

15

THE REST OF ACT THREE

The Capulet mansion. The nurse tells Juliet that Tybalt has been killed and Romeo has been banished.

Later that night, Lord Capulet tells Paris that he can marry Juliet in three days' time.

Early the next morning. Romeo and Juliet have spent the night together, but now Romeo has to leave.

Lady Capulet tells Juliet that she is to marry Paris. Juliet is horrified.

Lord Capulet is furious. He tells Juliet that he will throw her out if she does not obey him.

The nurse tells Juliet to forget Romeo. Juliet feels she can no longer trust her.

'I'LL NOT BE FORSWORN': ACT THREE, THE ARGUMENT

This is a very dramatic scene. Lord Capulet is furious, Juliet is desperate.

- What other characters are on stage and how might they be feeling?
- A director advises the actors on how to play a scene. What would you tell the four actors involved in this scene of the play?

- Try to act out this short scene.
- First read through the scene carefully and discuss the meaning of the words. For example, what do you think Capulet means when he says 'My fingers itch' or Lady Capulet when she says, 'You are too hot.'
- It would be useful to have a copy of the scene that you could make notes on.

CAPULET
How now, wife,
Have you delivered to her our decree?

LADY CAPULET
Ay, sir, but she will none; she gives
  you thanks.
I would the fool were married to
  her grave.

CAPULET
Soft, take me with you, take me with
  you, wife.
How, will she none? Doth she not
  give us thanks?
Is she not proud? doth she not count
  her blest,
Unworthy as she is, that we have
  wrought
So worthy a gentleman to be her bride?
To go with Paris to Saint Peter's Church,
Or I will drag thee on a hurdle thither.
Out, you green-sickness carrion! out,
  you baggage!
You tallow-face!

LADY CAPULET
Fie, fie, what, are you mad?

JULIET
Good father, I beseech you on my knees,
Hear me with patience but to speak
  a word.

[She kneels down.]

CAPULET
Hang thee, young baggage,
  disobedient wretch!
I tell thee what: get thee to church
  a'Thursday,
Or never after look me in the face.
Speak not, reply not, do not answer me!
My fingers itch. Wife, we scarce
  thought us blest
That God had lent us but this only child,
But now I see this one is one too much,
And that we have a curse in having her.
Out on her, hilding!

[continued on next page.]

NURSE
God in heaven bless her!
You are to blame, my lord, to rate her so.

CAPULET
And why, my Lady Wisdom? Hold your tongue, Good Prudence, smatter with your gossips, go.

NURSE
I speak no treason.

CAPULET
O God-i-goden!

NURSE
May not one speak?

CAPULET
Peace, you mumbling fool! Utter your gravity o'er a gossip's bowl, For here we need it not.

LADY CAPULET
You are too hot.

CAPULET
God's bread, it makes me mad! Day, night, work, play,
Alone, in company, still my care hath been
To have her matched; and having now provided
A gentleman of noble parentage,
Of fair demesnes, youthful and nobly ligned,
Stuffed, as they say, with honourable parts,
Proportioned as one's thought would wish a man,
And then to have a wretched puling fool,
A whining mammet, in her fortune's tender,
To answer 'I'll not wed, I cannot love;
I am too young, I pray you pardon me.'
But and you will not wed, I'll pardon you:
Graze where you will, you shall not house with me.

HELP

Think about directions for the actors. Think about how they should say their lines and the actions needed. If they all just stood still and said their lines it might be a very dull scene.

Watch as many versions on video of this scene as you can and compare your ideas to these.

Work in a group of four and act out this scene.
Try saying the lines in different ways.

Does an actor always have to shout to show anger?
Words whispered fiercely can be very effective.

Don't forget Lady Capulet and the Nurse. Although they don't say as much in this scene, they are still on stage. What should they be doing while the others are speaking?

- Using your notes, write up your advice for the four actors playing this scene. Explain how they should be behaving and why. How should they say particular lines?

- Include sketches or illustrations to show your actors what you mean.

PROBLEM PAGE

- Romeo and Juliet are in big trouble. How can they solve their problems?
- Fill in the gaps on a photocopy of their letters to a problem page.
- Then write a reply to both giving your advice. What *should* they do?

Dear problem page,

I am a young man from a good family who lives in V_____ . Yesterday I met the girl of my dreams and fell in love. Her name is J_____ . So why is this a problem you may be asking. Well _____ .

Today we got married in secret. The only people who know are F_____ _____ and the n_____ . Everything seemed to be going well until I was on my way home after the wedding. My new wife's cousin, who is called T_____ , challenged me to a duel. He is still angry about me gatecrashing his family's party. At first I told him _____ . He wouldn't leave me alone and we had a big fight. He killed by best friend M_____ , and then I killed T_____ .

I ran from the scene but when the Prince arrived he said _____ .

What should I do? I can't bear to live without my love but I am not allowed to stay. Yours desperately, Romeo

---

Dear problem page,

I am _____ years old and live in V_____ with my parents. Yesterday I did something in secret that I know they won't like. I _____ .

I love him so much even though we met for the first time at _____ . We talked at my window and he arranged for us to be married. I love him even though he is a M_____ and the enemy of my family.

Now there has been a fight and my cousin T_____ has been killed by R _____ my husband. I will miss my cousin but I know it could have been the other way around. My husband has been banished and left for Mantua this morning after spending the night with me.

To make matters worse, my father has just told me that I must marry a man called P_____ . I can't tell him about my husband and my father says that if I don't go through with this marriage he will _____ . My Nurse has told me that she thinks I should _____ . Everything is such a mess and I am so unhappy. What should I do? Yours sadly, Juliet

---

ACT FOUR

Juliet asks Friar Lawrence for his help, and he gives her a drug that will make her seem dead.

Juliet returns home and tells her father that she will marry Paris.

Juliet drinks the drug.

The next morning the nurse finds Juliet who seems to be dead.

ON THE HOT SEAT

- Put the following characters on the **hot seat**. What would each of them say about Juliet's death?

1 The Nurse

2 Lord Capulet (Juliet's father)

3 Lady Capulet (Juliet's mother)

4 Paris (the man Juliet's father wanted her to marry)

Use the prompt cards below to help you.

THE NURSE

- Has known Juliet since she was a baby.
- Thinks Juliet always follows her advice.
- Was the first to find Juliet dead. How did she feel? It was supposed to be Juliet's wedding day, and the Nurse had always wanted to see Juliet married.

LORD CAPULET

- Juliet is his only child.
- They had recently argued about her marriage to Paris.
- Juliet had said sorry and had agreed to do as he wished.

- The wedding must now be turned into a funeral.

LADY CAPULET

- Turned her back on Juliet when she argued with her father.
- Offered to help her last night but Juliet turned her down.

- Was married young and thought it was a good idea.

PARIS

- Loves Juliet and has wanted to marry her for some time, although he doesn't know her very well.
- This was to be the happiest day of his life.
- He will never forget her and wants to put flowers on her grave every day.

FRIAR LAWRENCE'S PLAN

Tape or write Friar Lawrence's letter to Romeo explaining his plan. The points below will help you.

1 Juliet to take potion that will make her seem dead.

2 The potion will last for 42 hours.

3 The wedding will have to be cancelled.

4 She will be buried in the Capulet tomb.

5 I will send a letter to Romeo explaining the plan.

6 Romeo will return from exile and be there when Juliet wakes up.

7 Romeo will take Juliet away with him.

8 I'm the only person who knows about their plan.

ACT FIVE

Romeo's servant tells Romeo that Juliet is dead. Friar Lawrence's letter never got to him.

Outside the Capulet tomb, Romeo is discovered by Paris. They fight.

Paris is killed and Romeo finds Juliet's body. He drinks the poison.

Seconds later, Juliet awakes. Friar Lawrence hears noises outside and runs away.

O happy dagger! This is thy sheath; there rust, and let me die.

Romeo and Juliet are found dead.

The Capulets and Montagues agree to end their quarrel.

FOCUS ON ROMEO

You have watched the whole play. You have worked on the activities in the first part of this book. Now use the 'Focus On' sheets on the following pages to look at some of the characters more closely.

You could split into groups to look at different characters and then report back.

At the end of Act One

• Fill in the following information about Romeo:
  – First name:
  – Family name:
  – Age:
  – Parents:
  – Friends:

After Act Two

• Think about the fact that Romeo has married Juliet. It has all been very quick. How well can they know each other?

• What is it that attracts Romeo to Juliet?

After Act Three

• Look at the words below which describe Romeo. Write down the line numbers and quotations that tell you what he is like.
  – *young*: Act 1, Scene 5, line 63 – 'Young Romeo is it?'
  – *moody*: Act 1, Scene 1, line 124 – 'with his deep sighs'
  – *love-sick*:
  – *determined*:

• Can you think of any other words to describe Romeo?

After Act Five

• Think about what happened to Romeo.

• Put the following sentences in order to describe the events of the last few days:

  1 Romeo is in love with Rosaline.

  2 Romeo marries Juliet.

  3 Romeo meets Juliet at the Capulet party.

  4 Romeo kills Tybalt.

  5 Romeo takes poison and dies.

  6 Romeo lives in exile.

• Now match each sentence with a quotation from the list below.

  A 'Thus with a kiss I die.'

  B 'I do love a woman.'

  C 'Take the "villain" back again.'

  D 'There is no world without Verona.'

  E 'It is enough I may call her mine.'

  F 'Did my heart love till now?'

FOCUS ON JULIET

At the end of Act One

- Fill in the following information about Juliet:
  - First name:
  - Family name:
  - Age:
  - Parents:
  - Friends:

After Act Two

- Think about the fact that Juliet has married Romeo. It has all been very quick. How well does Juliet know Romeo? What sort of person is Juliet? Should she have talked to her parents?

After Act Three

- Decide which of the words below best describe Juliet. Write down the line numbers and quotations that tell you what she is like.

  - *young*: Act 1, Scene 3 – 'Come Lammas-eve at night she will be fourteen.'
  - *in love*: Act 2, Scene 2 – 'O Romeo, Romeo, wherefore art thou Romeo?'
  - *determined*:
  - *honest*:

- Can you think of any other words to describe Juliet?

After Act Five

- Think about what has happened to Juliet.

- Put the following sentences in order to describe the events of the last few days:

  1 Juliet tries to avoid her marriage to Paris.

  2 Juliet marries Romeo.

  3 Juliet kills herself.

  4 Juliet mourns the death of Tybalt.

  5 Juliet meets Romeo.

- Now match these quotations to the events described above:

  A 'My only love sprung from my only hate.'

  B 'Tell me how I may prevent it?'

  C 'Tybalt's death was woe enough.'

  D 'O happy dagger! This is thy sheath.'

  E 'Till Holy Church incorporate two in one.'

FOCUS ON FRIAR LAWRENCE

Friar Lawrence has married Romeo and Juliet. Why would he agree to do this?

- Which of the statements below do you think explain his actions?

  1 He married them because Romeo asked him to.

  2 The nurse thought it was a good idea.

  3 He thought it was a good idea.

  4 He thought it would bring an end to the feuding of the families.

- Can you think of any other reasons?

- What sort of person do you think the Friar is? Can you find any evidence to suggest that he is:
  - *wise*
  - *interfering*
  - *stupid*
  - *kind-hearted*

- The Friar's actions are very important to the play. Put in order the actions taken by the Friar:

  1 He sends Romeo a letter.

  2 He marries Romeo and Juliet.

  3 He gives Juliet a potion to take.

  4 He arranges Juliet's funeral.

- Now match these quotations with the events above:

  A 'In one respect I'll thy assistant be.'

  B 'Take thou this vial.'

  C 'Every one prepare to follow this fair corse unto her grave.'

  D 'I'll send a friar with speed to Mantua with letters to thy lord.'

FOCUS ON THE NURSE

We can tell that the nurse knows Juliet well by the things she says about her:

– 'The prettiest babe that e'er I nursed.'

– She 'can tell her age unto an hour' and hopes that 'I might live to see thee married once, I have my wish.'

Act 1 Scene 3

- Look at these words which describe the nurse. Can you give examples to support what you say?
    - *kind*: (takes messages for Juliet)
    - *funny*: (tells stories and laughs at rude jokes)
    - *sensible*:
    - *hardworking*:
    - *trustworthy*:
    - *loyal*:

Act 3 Scene 5

Juliet turns to the nurse for advice. She tells Juliet, 'I think it best you married with the County, O, he's a lovely gentleman! Romeo's a dishclout to him.'

- What might she be thinking when she says this? Why has she helped Juliet up to this point? What has changed?

- The nurse plays an important part in the story. Put in order the actions taken by the nurse:

    1 The nurse finds Juliet 'dead' on her wedding day.

    2 She brings news of Tybalt's death and Romeo's banishment.

    3 She acts as messenger between Juliet and Romeo.

    4 She advises Juliet to marry Paris.

    5 She tries to protect Juliet from her father's anger.

    6 She arranges for Romeo to spend the night with Juliet.

- Now match these quotations to the events described above:

    A 'My young lady bid me enquire you out.'

    B 'Hark ye, your Romeo be here tonight.'

    C 'I think it best you married with County.'

    D 'Help, help! My lady's dead!'

    E 'Tybalt is gone and Romeo banished.'

    F 'You are to blame, my lord, to rate her so.'

TIME LINE

- Ask your teacher for a copy of the timeline bottle on the opposite page.

• As you read through the play, look at the list of events below. They are not in the correct order. Fill in the timeline bottle with the events below, and put them in the right order.

- Juliet is discovered 'dead' in the morning
- Romeo leaves Juliet at dawn
- The marriage is in the afternoon
- Romeo kills Tybalt
- Romeo returns to Verona, kills Paris, drinks poison
- Street fight
- Romeo finds out that Juliet is 'dead'
- Invitations sent out
- Juliet's wedding to Paris brought forward to Wednesday
- The two feuding families make peace
- Juliet goes to see Friar Lawrence
- Juliet is told she is to marry Paris
- Balcony scene
- Romeo and Juliet meet at the party
- Juliet fakes her death
- Romeo spends the night with his new wife
- Romeo visits Friar Lawrence
- Funeral
- Juliet's marriage to Paris is arranged by Capulet
- Juliet takes the Friar's potion at bedtime.

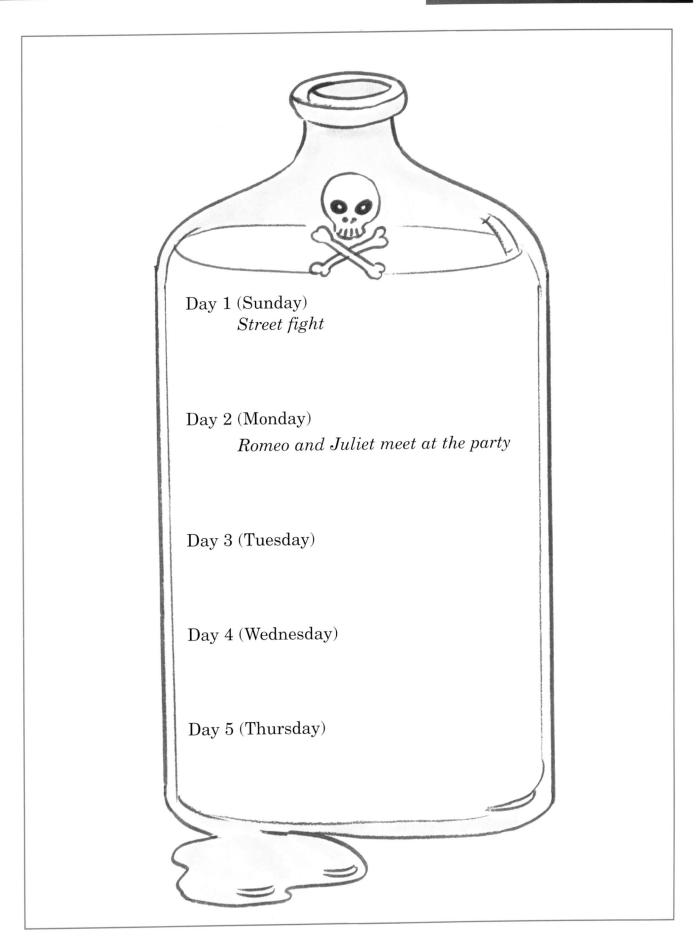

Day 1 (Sunday)
Street fight

Day 2 (Monday)
Romeo and Juliet meet at the party

Day 3 (Tuesday)

Day 4 (Wednesday)

Day 5 (Thursday)

WHO IS TO BLAME?

There is a public enquiry after Romeo and Juliet have been found dead.

- Look at all the characters in turn and decide how much they are to blame for what has happened. You will need to present the evidence at the enquiry. Some suggestions are given on the prompt cards below.

- What other evidence and reasons can you find? You could look at the servants, and even 'fate'.

1 LORD CAPULET

Insisted Juliet marry the County Paris. Wouldn't listen to his daughter.

'Get thee to church a'Thursday, or never after look me in the face.'

2 LADY CAPULET

Turned her back on her daughter. Supported her husband.

'Talk not to me, for I'll not speak a word.'

3 THE NURSE

Encouraged Juliet to meet and marry Romeo, and then betrayed her.

'I think it best you marry with the County.'

4 FRIAR LAWRENCE

Agreed to marry Romeo and Juliet in secret. Gave Juliet the drugs but would not stay to help her in the tomb.

'I dare no longer stay.'

5 APOTHECARY

Sold poison to Romeo, even though it was against the law.

'Such mortal drugs I have.'

6 PRINCE ESCALUS

Banished Romeo. Did not stop the fighting in time.

'And for that offence immediately we do exile him hence.'

7 LORD & LADY MONTAGUE

Continued the feud. Did they do enough to find out what their son's problem was?

'I neither know it nor can learn of him.'

8 PARIS

Kept asking Capulet if he could marry Juliet.

'But now, my lord, what say you to my suit.'

9 TYBALT

Always looking for a fight. Killed Mercutio. Wants revenge on Romeo.

'Thou art a villain.'

10 BENVOLIO

It was his idea to gatecrash the Capulet party.

'Examine other beauties.'

11 MERCUTIO

Fights Tybalt.

'Make it a word and a blow.'

12 ROMEO AND JULIET

Knew their parents wouldn't approve of their marriage. Involved others in their secrets.

- Hold the public enquiry. Present evidence against each character. Questions and comments can be made after each person has presented their character.

- Put the characters in order of responsibility by cutting out the cards and arranging them. Who is most to blame for the deaths of Romeo and Juliet?

WHAT NEXT?

In this unit you have looked carefully at the play *Romeo and Juliet*. You have also followed the plot and understood how events have led to the deaths of the characters Romeo and Juliet. You have used role-play to help you think about the characters and how they might feel at key moments in the play, and you have completed tasks to help you understand what is happening. If you have watched a performance of the play on stage or video you will be able to see how it all fits together.

You may want to continue your work by completing some or all of the following extension tasks.

- Imagine you are going to produce the play *Romeo and Juliet*. Design costumes and sets for your production and think about who you would get to play the parts. Would it be a traditional or modern version?

- Design a theatre programme for the play. Your teacher may have some you could look at. You could include some background to the play and Shakespeare himself, which might involve some research in the library.

- Produce a simplified version of the story for a younger child to introduce them to Shakespeare. Use your own work to help you get the sequence of events correct.